Alternatives...

A Journey to New Hope

by Teri Prock

DORRANCE PUBLISHING CO
EST. 1920
PITTSBURGH, PENNSYLVANIA 15238

Dorrance Publishing Co
585 Alpha Drive
Pittsburgh, PA 15238
Visit our website at *www.dorrancebookstore.com*

ISBN: 979-8-89211-410-3
eISBN: 979-8-89211-908-5

Alternatives...

A Journey to New Hope

FOREWORD

This author holds your attention from beginning to end. Throughout her book, she shows that good and bad situations happen to each one of us. It is what we choose to do with each situation that can either inhibit our growth or make us grow stronger and mold us into the person we are today.

She has a simple yet unique way of writing that gives you the knowledge and desire to seek your own path to good alternatives.

Mary Cook

About the Front and Back Cover Illustrations

When beginning your journey into this book, a person's self-esteem, self-worth, and confidence are probably at a low. However, after reading and doing the work here, I pray that you will have become closer to the confident, worthy person you know you can be.

All poems within this book were written by Teri Prock, previously known as Teri Gambill.

This book is dedicated to

L. Maxine Rookstool "my grandmother,"

Who loved me with all her heart,

Who never painted a picture of life being fair,

Who gave me the basics for a good foundation in Christ.

TABLE OF CONTENTS

Special Acknowledgements

I give God the praise and the glory for using me as the vessel to bring this message to you.

I thank my spiritual support team for the help they gave me in keeping with the spirit of my message.

In the physical realm, I thank my husband Mike, who loves me unconditionally, believes in me, has supported my every endeavor and instilled within me the understanding that "it's okay to be me and to stand firm in my beliefs."

Please, *before you jump to conclusions thinking this is a "church" or "Bible-thumping book," rest assured it's **NOT!***

Acknowledgements

The last few years have been a spiritual journey that I have greatly enjoyed. During this time, I discovered that God has provided us with many tools to help us along our life's mission. I learned what is right for me, and that it is okay not to conform to tradition as set by society. This in turn has immensely increased my faith and inner strength.

My life has been filled with happiness and many lessons and I would like to express my gratitude and acknowledge…

My loving parents, Gordon and Mary Cook. Thank you for being you and instilling within me my morals, values, and beliefs. I love you both very much!

To three exceptional women, my daughters, Jennifer, Joslyn, and Kristin. I am so grateful for your unconditional love and so thankful that all three of you have the courage to be yourselves, no matter the circumstance or situation. To their husbands—thank you for providing for, supporting, and encouraging them on their endeavors.

I acknowledge my devoted friends Cathy Smith Lovin, Mary Bryant, Dot Veristain, and Casey Cheek for their strength, love, support, and spiritual skills within my life. They have been the perfect examples of true friends no matter the distance or amount of time between visits.

Dot—You immediately feel her bubbly energy. She always has a smile, and her energy is like that of a child's. She may be little, but don't let that fool you; she is like a stick of dynamite when it comes to those she loves. Thank you, Dot, for just being you!

Casey—Casey has a persona that automatically demands respect. You immediately sense and feel the spirit that radiates within her, while at the same time the energy in a room just snaps with her presence. Thank you, Casey, for demonstrating how to live within the Spirit with no doubts and teaching me the "rules for being human," along with being my sister in spirit.

PREFACE

This book is about choosing a positive way to rise above our present situations as well as the many trials of life.

My intention is to show how faith as an alternative helped me (along with others I know) to learn how to stop running from their problems, how to stop repeating the same patterns, as well as the importance of forgiveness. There are many good alternatives offered within this world. We just need to be willing to find and participate in the ones that are right for us.

It is my heartfelt desire that should this book help only one person, I have achieved my goal.

Of the many names we use for that Power Which Is Greater Than Ourselves (God, Goddess, Buddha, Wankan Tanka, Great Spirit, etc.), for the simplicity of writing I have chosen God in male form. It is not my intention to offend anyone in their beliefs. When referring to the term spirituality it's meaning is of spiritual character, quality, or nature. The words negatives, negativity, and positives are not meant to be judgmental. They are used as well for the simplicity of writing. Negatives meaning that which is an attitude or thought characterized by doubt, question, or resistance. Positives meaning that which is right, good, confident, or certain.

I have used my life experiences as examples, knowing also that many people have experienced considerably worse than I have.

*I encourage those who read this book **to participate in the exercises** with the intention of having fun, as well as keeping an open mind.*

INTRODUCTION

When we are born, we arrive as our True Self. We come here as innocent, loving, happy, forgiving, and accepting human beings. We carry no judgements. We also arrive with a built-in defense mechanism, our intuition, i.e. the voice of God. WE come prepared to let negatives and positives flow through us.

Upon our arrival, we get the opportunity to begin the never-ending school of life, moving from one playground to the next and experiencing many of life's different lessons, as well as being able to play on a variety of life's playground equipment. Examples: merry-go-round (chasing your tail), slide (life's slippery slide), roller coaster (life's continuous ups and downs).

During our adolescent years, our personalities, characteristics, beliefs, and attitudes are being shaped by our parents, families, society, churches, and friends. As adolescents, a good majority of us are taught God, and our parents love us unconditionally and always will; that our families love us; that families stick together through thick and thin. We are to support one another 100 percent and to trust our parents with **everything** and **anything**. If they are not available, to go to the police.

As we grow older, our thoughts and actions lead us to a point where we want to establish our own identities and make our own decisions. We start to trust our friends instead of family. Why? They *understand* us! We are convinced that they will always be there. At this time in our life, we've also had the opportunity to experience a mixture of learning lessons on the playground of life, and for many of us, faith was left behind. With this in mind, I would like to share some of my own life's lessons.

Chapter 1
Childhood

Let's face it, our elementary years are rough. Each experience we encounter makes us stronger and it's these experiences that prepare us for adulthood, yet, as children, *we tend to believe life is unfair.* The following are some examples of my own personal experiences when I felt life to be unfair.

I was born with epilepsy and later blessed with grand mal seizures. I never knew when one was coming on. I remember having them in the bus line, at school, during family functions, and friend's houses. At times I felt humiliated, embarrassed, and ashamed. Because of the medications I had to take, school was very difficult. I passed with below-average scores. I felt as if I was an embarrassment to my siblings. I just knew in my heart I was a huge disappointment to my parents, and I tried very hard to make up for this by being responsible, taking on more responsibility than a child should. The most important thing my parents did for me was to treat me just like my brother and sisters. They did not let my seizures hinder me in any way.

My parents worked fulltime and very hard to provide a good home for us. My dad treated my mom with respect and doted on her like a queen because he loved her. He was grateful for her presence as his wife, and Mom in turn did the same for Dad.

After establishing that we (us kids) were old enough to be left on our own, it became our responsibility for the household chores, dinners, baked goods for all our lunches, along with getting our homework done.

Because the oldest child syndrome had been placed upon me, sibling rivalry was a <u>major daily issue</u>. Needless to say my siblings and I were extremely resentful and jealous of each other. Did we fight? You bet we did! However, in spite of all the above, we were a close family.

Looking back at my childhood, I see it in a much different light. To be honest, I have to say I had a good childhood. However, (like most children) I felt life was *very* unfair.

At the age of ten, my mother invited the Mormon (LDS) missionaries to come and witness to our family. The results were that my sisters, brother, and myself were baptized as LDS. My heart said it was the right thing to do. In looking back, my decision to be baptized was so my parents would be proud of me. Therefore, my decision was not made for the right reason.

I had previously gone to church with friends and family of other denominations. Along with Christianity, my heart was drawn to Native American spirituality and culture; my outdoor involvement with campfire girls is where it truly began, along with all the camping and outdoor sports my family participated in whenever possible.

My grandparents, who attended the Presbyterian Church, were avid Christians, and my grandmother was very bold in her beliefs. She would read the Bible and quote its verses to me every chance she got, just so she could let me know that Mormonism was not **the** way to go. She did this lovingly, of course, as she was a very loving and kind spirit.

After sixth grade, we didn't go to church often. I came to a point where I did not know what religion to believe in. However, I was knowledgeable enough to know that when my heart felt good about something, it was usually true. I found that this applied to all services I attended. Therefore, my observation was that there was good in every church.

As I grew older, I kept searching; something was still missing. There was something more pulling at me, and I continued seeking truth in each. It took years to arrive at a point where I felt fulfilled (whole).

FOOD FOR THOUGHT

- When you put two people together (marriage) who have been taught two entirely different ways of life, throw in a lack of communication skills and experience, life becomes tough; add children to this marriage and life for everyone becomes tougher yet!

- The parent role is difficult. People do as they have been taught through their parents or the life lessons they have experienced. We are not supplied with manuals on "How to Be a Parent" or, better, "How to Deal with Our Parents." We all do the best we can or know how. Because that's all we know. Because parenting is so overwhelming, spirituality gets left out.

- Most parents do not stop to think about *how their reaction* to something their child has said or done will affect the child emotionally, or how said child will then form a *life-long* pattern for themselves concerning said issue. So many parents assume their children interpret things the same as they do *as an adult*.

- Too often parents refuse or do not know how to take responsibility for their actions or situations, and the child gets the blame. Ex: A parent says, "We didn't have **any** bills until the kids came along." The children will then blame themselves for the financial burdens in the family. Whose fault is it that the children arrived? Not the children!

- As parents, we need to step into the shoes of our children, come down to their level, and, most of all communicate, communicate, communicate, making sure they understand clearly what we mean.

- Childhood is hard. As children, our feelings and emotions are extremely intense.

- Along with these feelings come an extraordinary sense of right and wrong. This sense of right and wrong makes it even tougher when abuse is present. What do I know about abuse, you ask? My experience came later in life.

- It's too bad most parents are not educated on parenting before they become parents. Along with the fact that they *"have the ability to choose to break the parenting cycle"*_that has been handed down to them for centuries. People have the right to make corrections for the better.

REFLECTION EXERCISE

- What did you learn from your childhood experiences? Ex: courage, confidence, patience, endurance, love, etc.
- What did these experiences have to do with who you are today?
- How would you describe yourself today?
- What did these experiences teach you about handling challenging situations?
- How did these experiences teach you to be creative?
- Did you have a spiritual affiliation as a child? If yes, are you willing to build on them today?
- As a parent, do you give thought to the words and actions you use with your child and how they will alter your child's growth?
- Do you want to be a slave to your memories and remain tied to the derogatory lies concerning your self-worth and self-esteem, or do you want to simply see them as life lessons that, although painful, have helped you gain strength and character to become who you are today?
- Do any of your answers surprise you? How so?

CHAPTER 2
Life Lessons

Like most people, I got caught up in the game of life. During my teen years, I thought life was hell at home. I began to seek my independence, wanting to take control of my own life. I knew I was a responsible person; everyone told me so. Bottom line, "I did not want to live at home anymore."

I married for the first time at age sixteen. We were *young* and *immature*! My husband treated me with disrespect and as a sex symbol trophy. Along with this, he was demanding and controlling. He was known for his belittling ways.

If this was love, I didn't want any part of it. You cannot love someone when you have the need to own or control them.

I began to look to God for strength to get me through the days and nights. However, I was still weak in that area. At one point my grandma came to stay with us for a week and at that time she informed me, *"You can be or do anything through the power of Jesus Christ who strengthens you,"* Philippians 4:13. Within my heart, I knew this to be true.

We had two beautiful daughters during our marriage, and I loved being a mother. But I did not want my children to be raised in this mindset or environment, so I packed our daughters and left. I got off this merry-go-round.

Later, I again tried marriage. My husband dearly loved my girls; he literally adopted them as his own. He was a wonderful father and a good provider—money was never an issue. However, we had completely different tastes in lifestyles and hobbies. We had nothing in common.

I began to realize I did not love him the way he deserved; our relationship was missing many characterizations that make a marriage. When I became pregnant, it almost caused a divorce. He was happy with two children and a wife; as far as he was concerned he did not need more. We had been married for six years when I decided to leave the negativity of this merry-go-round! I had been on the rebound when we met. I was not in love with him. Once again, I married for the wrong reason. This playground was worse than the first. I also realized that God had been a major missing piece in this relationship as well.

FOOD FOR THOUGHT

- Love has many different meanings. We (the human race) tend to justify our reasons or meanings for what fits our situations at the time. We need to truly look at what love really means before making life altering choices. For each choice we make has a consequence good or bad
- The difference between loving someone and being in love with them is we love everyone the same, but we choose one person to be our *partner* in life, and in that partnership, in *most areas* there is unity. In short, we love everyone the same, but we do not choose to have everyone as our partner.
- Using my ex-husband for an example, I loved him when he was my partner, I still love him as a person, I just choose not to have him as my partner. There was no unity in our relationship.
- Physical attraction is often mistaken for love. People's physical needs override the importance of companionship and commitment, a need for a lifetime partnership. Physical attraction is simply fulfilling a sexual need, nothing more. This attraction rarely lasts very long; in the end, it most often leaves a person feeling incomplete, with possible feelings of guilt. Just because we have sex with someone does not mean that they love us, nor does it mean we love them.

CHAPTER 3
Another One of Life's Lessons

Finally, I reached a point where I thought I really knew what I needed and wanted out of life for my girls and myself.

Quite by accident, I came across my best friend from high school. We had always felt something for each other but were not willing to put our friendship at risk by getting involved in a relationship. He had been married and divorced once, and during his marriage came two children, a boy and girl.

Coming from a strict Christian background, he knew God and Jesus Christ. We married and joined our two families; I just knew that we could become a happy and loving family. A loving Christian family had always been my dream.

Because of our Christianity, I had myself excommunicated from the LDS Church. Mormonism did not fit the beliefs I had acquired through the past few years.

I loved my husband and was *in love* with him and had married him for the right reasons. I knew deep in my heart that we could make it through anything. With Love and God on our side, what could go wrong?

You know the old saying "love is blind"! Ex: It did not take me long to realize that alcohol was a problem in our marriage. As it turned out, my husband was a workaholic and a borderline alcoholic, which left no room for family interaction.

All emotions within were turning me inside out. My girls weren't happy here, either. This was looking to be the worst ride yet! We didn't know when the next hill or turn was coming; therefore, it was difficult to jump off the roller coaster.

One day, after working a graveyard shift, and all the kids were off to school, there was a knock at my door. I opened the door to the sheriff and Children's Services! They informed me that my husband had been arrested on the job, and arrangements were being made for my children to live outside our home until further investigation could be done. I was *devastated*! My heart felt as if it had been yanked out of my chest. I asked, "Why? What is going on?" They would not answer my question, but they wanted answers from me. My in-laws arrived thirty minutes later. They wanted to know "what **I** had done to get their son thrown in jail." Everyone wanted answers, and I didn't have any, I was just as confused as they were! Everyone who thought they should be involved were judgmental, cruel, and rude.

Finally, I received an answer; my husband had been arrested for sexually abusing my two oldest daughters. *I went into shock!* I was told my daughters would receive a counselor, so they could learn to *cope and hopefully* be able to get on with their lives. I was not given the freedom to make any decisions concerning my daughters nor was I allowed to speak with my daughters, let alone give them a hug or tell them I love them, that everything would be all right. Not even when Children's Services brought them to the house to gather their things with the police there. I was not allowed to know where my daughters had been placed and I was served with a no-contact order against me until further notice.

I tried to continue working, but I could not get myself together. I had to work with the public and they knew us as a couple. I quit my job. I still had not been able to speak to my husband; he refused to see me, because he didn't know where I stood. I needed to pick up my husband's paycheck so I could pay our bills. His parents received his check. Our electricity was shut off for lack of payment, and I needed a place to stay. My in-laws said I could not stay with them, as they did not know if they could trust me.

Friends vanished into the woodwork, not wanting anything to do with our circumstances. My parents' house was full, therefore, not an option.

There was no other place to go, so I stayed in our home and made do with what I could.

Until I could speak with my husband and find out where he stood, I could not decide what I would, could, or even wanted to do.

In this mess of messes, our law enforcement, along with the DA's office, lost papers, never to be found. While my husband was sitting in jail, they issued a warrant for his arrest, for failure to appear in court. I remember thinking, "We are supposed to trust these people?" After being released on his own recognizance, my husband's attorney told him not to worry about appearing for the upcoming hearing because the courts had not notified him. For following his attorney's advice, he spent another week in jail.

I had no idea what the truth was. There were so many blatant mistakes being made that I was frantically trying to make sense of our situation. How could I believe our law officials, let alone my husband!

What kind of decision could I possibly make when I could not find a grain of truth in my foundation.

My husband received community service and five years of probation, along with counseling.

During this time, I realized my faith was wavering, and faith had been missing for quite some time within our marriage. Who was guiding our lives? Not God!

We decided that we wanted to keep our family together; I was willing to try. We made the decision to do our best to put our family back together. My husband had asked God for forgiveness and made the promise to change inside as well as out and agreed to continue to receive counseling. We could try and get through this.

My heart said God gives people *second chances*. My intuition was telling me this was what I needed to do as well. I knew my girls were receiving help, and they were good, strong young women who would live a good and prosperous life. I knew they could do it, for I had faith in my daughters. I prayed daily that all would be forgiven, so we would someday be the happy family. I knew in my heart we could be. I did not want to have to start over with my life again. Besides, I still loved my husband. However, my doubts were high, and I was strongly thinking about bailing from the relationship.

The State will tell you, "We try to keep families together." They literally tore mine apart. They informed me that I could no longer reside in my own home with my husband. His counselor instructed "for him to be able to complete his treatment, we had to separate for one year." ***They told me I had to leave!***

Stamina

Where was the counseling for the middle person, and at no cost? There wasn't any! There was help for the victims and the perpetrator, but not the middle person who had tried to hold everything together.

What were my alternatives: Alcohol? Drugs? Running? Suicide? Counseling? These alternatives did not appeal to me. There had to be another way. But what, where, when, who, or how? There was professional counseling, but they were affiliated with the *law*, and it cost *money* I did not have. They were human, too; would they let me down like the others had? Good possibility! The only other alternative I had was faith, and I had little knowledge of it. What little I did know would have to get me through.

Everyone had their opinions of **what** I needed to do and **how they** would handle my situation if they were in my shoes. Which reminds me of something my grandma used to say, "Never say you would do such and such until you have walked a mile in their shoes."

None of the advice sounded right or good. People would ask, "How can you forgive him, and how can you trust him after what he has done?" In my thoughts, I would add, "How can I trust anyone?" How could I forgive or trust the people that were against everything I had been taught and to believe in? They did not support what I chose to do, which was to be forgiving and try to work things out. My friends vanished. The law tore my family apart! Yes, my husband had to be stopped and needed to be punished for his actions. But why were the kids and I separated? Why were we the ones having to leave our home? Why did he get the privilege of remaining in our home?

All the things I had been taught and I had lived by went right out the window. I did not know where trust or love came in.

I would like to share my emotions at this time. I was scared to death! All I had ever done was waitressing, bartending, and sales. How was I going to support myself with three girls? I didn't even know yet *if* I was going to be able to get them back! I had no self-confidence, let alone self-worth. It was gone. *I was mad! Mad as hell!* I was hurt beyond any hurt I had ever felt in my whole life. I felt like I had fallen out of the top of a tree and hit every branch on my way down. I hurt inside and out. I felt betrayed by everyone except my kids. My attitude stunk, and I was getting nowhere. I really did not know if I wanted to live anymore. Life was one big pile of shit! I kept asking myself, "What did we do to deserve this?" I finally concluded that I could either sink or swim; continue this way and wallow in self-pity, or I could change my attitude and follow my heart.

I had only my heart and my intuition to guide me. How could I be forgiving? Again, my intuition was telling me this was what I needed to do. However, just because we forgive someone **does not mean we condone what they have done.** When we forgive someone, it is just as much for us as it is for them. For us it is a necessity. *It enables our hearts and minds to go on, instead of wasting energy dwelling on the negatives of life.*

Where would focusing on the negatives get me? *Nowhere!* What would focusing on the negatives get me? *Nothing!* Nothing but more negativity. My past was full of negatives. My heart began talking to me in a big way, and I began to listen!

The first step I took was to ask Children's Services "what will it take in order for my daughters and I to be able to live together?" I was told I had to find an apartment or a house where *ONLY* the four of us would reside, and my husband was not to come around for any reason. In the beginning, no one had informed me that I had this right. It would have been nice to know at the beginning of this mess.

My daughters and I moved into a three-bedroom apartment for low-income families. Each daughter had her own bedroom, because it was important to me for them to have their own space. I split the living room in half with a couple of bed sheets and placed my bed there. This was all the space I needed if my daughters were able to be with me.

Circumstances Beyond Their Control

Circumstances beyond their control,
Mother and daughters now on their own,
Scraping by month to month,
To meet the needs of many.
Lord, please help with self-discipline,
There is more responsibility than
They want to hold.
The trials of life have left them cold.
Lord, please help them rise and be bold.
Thank you, Lord, for
Giving them each other to hold!

Written by
Teri Gamibill
March 15, 1994

Marital Separation

Am I capable of going it alone?
I've never made decisions on my own.
The trials of being a single parent
Now are very apparent.
How do my children feel?
Do they believe our situation is real?
Where will money come from?
We've nil for income.
Should we go on welfare?
Or should I opt for a career?
What kind of job could I find
That wouldn't keep us in a bind?
Should I go to college?
Soon I hope to cross that bridge.
I have two cars with which to play rotation.
Separation has many pitfalls,
One being, no one to call.

Written by
Teri Gambill
January 15, 1994

I received a grant to attend college and proceeded to enroll in Human Services. I felt called to become a counselor and work with women. During this time, I began having seizures once again, as a result of stress and not taking good care of myself. A year later it was better to drop out of college, due to too many seizures.

I went to CAPECO, an agency that places people accordingly with a job through a program called Jobs Plus. Through this program I received a job with EOAF, an in-house alcohol and drug rehabilitation treatment center. I was hired as children's coordinator and counselor trainee for the women's house.

Only by the grace of God was I placed in such employment. Mind you, I had only one year of college. I did not have a master's or Bachelor of Arts degree in education, let alone psychiatry.

During this time, my oldest daughter came home from school and informed me that she had come across a quote that she was going to live by, "*Shame on my parents for who I am today, but shame on me if I stay that way.*" I adopted and applied this to our situation. If my daughter could be positive, so could I.

When I talked with God that night, I thanked Him for the blessings I did have. I also asked Him for help with a few things, mainly a change in attitude.

Later, after journaling, my mind kept recalling Bible verses. Philippians 4:13: *I can do all things through Christ who strengthens me.* Proverbs 3:5, 6: *Trust in the Lord with all thine heart and lean not unto your own understanding.* Hebrews 11:1: *Now faith is the substance of things hoped, the evidence of things not seen.* Hebrews 13:8: *Jesus Christ the same yesterday, today and forever.* Somewhere in the back of my mind I had stored these verses. I was not familiar with my Bible. I guess the readings and quotes from my grandma stayed with me. I realized after journaling that I had been relying on these verses all along.

Putting my trust in God did not hurt, loving Him did not hurt and letting Him guide me did not hurt either. My grandma taught me this also, "*God never changes, but the human race does continuously; God won't let us down, we let ourselves down because of the choices we make or have made.*"

Please, do not misunderstand what I am saying. Placing my faith in a Higher Power gave me HOPE, as well as a different focus point. This was a good alternative for me and has been for others as well. God was answering my prayer for a changing attitude.

I began to get stronger day by day. I loved my work, being able to help the women and their children start new lives for themselves.

The center started sending me to trainings and workshops so that in time I could possibly get my CADC I (Certified Alcohol and Drug Counselor). Cultural differences happened to be one of the specific trainings.

Once again, my beliefs began to change. I was learning that along with Christianity, there were many other truths on this earth to learn about.

Due to a binding contract, requiring me to report any wage increase with the low-income housing facility, I turned in my earnings report for my land-lord's attention. This resulted in my rent going from fifty dollars a month to six hundred dollars a month. My landlord then gave me thirty days to either pay six hundred dollars or move out with my daughters.

Again, I was devasted; then I got really mad and said to myself, *Damn it! Where is the justice in this? I have followed every stinking rule to the letter in order to keep my family together and rise above our situation, only to be kicked in the teeth. Something is very wrong with this picture!*

Furthermore, no one seemed to care about the children who were stuck in this situation. Their world was being knocked out from underneath them once again as well. They did not have a choice and were trusting me to make things right!

In looking at the situation, I brought home eight hundred dollars a month. Rent was six hundred dollars, leaving me with two hundred to pay the used car payment, insurance, household items, utilities, phone, gas, food, and school expenses. There was not enough, no matter how I figured and scrimped. This dilemma left me with three options:

- Find a house big enough for the four of us, be it a two- or three-bedroom for four hundred dollars or less. Continue to work on putting my family back together.
- Take a one-bedroom apartment and send my daughters back to live with their dad. Continue to work on putting my family back together.
- Go back to my husband, send my two oldest daughters to live with their dad, and take my youngest with me, continuing to work on putting my family back together.

I went in search of housing, only to find that due to college starting two months prior, all rentals had been taken. All landlords I spoke with informed that this happens every year at this time.

This left me with only the choice of going back to live with my husband. Meaning, I would have to send my two oldest daughters to live with their dad and his new family. I asked myself, *How many more let downs can we handle?*

God and I were going to have a long talk, and He was going to listen! I had questions, and I wanted answers. I let Him know my heartfelt opinions as well. I received the silent treatment. (Just an FYI, telling God what to do doesn't work, I had just tried it). Truthfully, I wasn't willing to listen. I wanted things my way and rain on everything and everybody else! When telling my daughters what had to be done, I hid my true feelings concerning our situation (they worried about me enough because of my seizures). I had no other option. Also, I tried to convince them that this was the best way for all of us, and in the end it would all be worked out.

My daughters had been my rock, my support. They my priority, although my actions (having to move back with my husband) stated differently. As far as they were concerned, I chose a man over my own flesh and blood. If I was going to work at getting my family back together, I truthfully had no other option. So, I did what I had to do. In so doing, my heart was being ripped out of my chest, *never* to be fully repaired again. It was also evident that because of my decision, any respect I once had from my daughters was severely tarnished. The next few years brought more trials and drastic changes for all of us; included in this was that my husband had committed to the Lord, stopped drinking, stopped smoking and chewing, and we were working together to reunite our family. Spirituality was once more a part of our relationship.

One year later, to the day, we were able to have association as a "whole" family! It was at this time I realized one very major thing. In forgiving my husband and in wanting so badly for us to be reunited as a family again, I had forgotten to consider "what will happen when he gets off probation, what then? Will he continue his spirituality? Will he stay away from alcohol?"

Why would he not? It had been five years. I truly believed everything would finally work out.

The very day he got off probation, my husband went directly to the store, bought a case of beer and a can of chewing tobacco and a pack of Marlboro cigarettes, and decided it was party time. Any spirituality that had been evident disappeared. Again, let me say he HAD NOT touched it in five years…. In short, life drastically changed once again…

I would come home from work to find parties that should not have been taking place at all! There were two children who had to get up and go to school the next morning. Of course, all his work buddies were more than helpful in helping him celebrate. These parties would last till one or two in the morning and were happening at the very least four nights a week and on the weekends. I have to say the weekend parties were the worst!

Each time I would refuse to have any part of them, I would hear "you're no fun anymore!" I had *never* been a drinker, what was the difference now? My question was, "Hadn't he learned anything?" I had several, very valid reasons for not wanting alcohol in our home, one being that alcohol had played a big part in him getting arrested in the first place, and, second, his actions could have lost me my job, among many other very important things. The partying influenced a double standard between my work and home life. I was beginning to feel as if I was losing my sanity. *This was not okay with me!*

I had overcome being pushed off the slide as a child, getting nauseous on the merry-go-round's wheel of negativity, along with falling from a tree. I had worked hard and come too far and I refused to go backwards!

Finally, I chose not to live this way. I had loved, forgiven, and trusted, only to have it **all** destroyed, over and over and over again. By loving, forgiving, and trusting the many, many, many times that I had, I could honestly say and honestly believed in my heart that I had given this marriage above and beyond my all. For six years I exhausted myself, trying and believing it could work. We were divorced after thirteen and a half years. We parted ways in a friendly manner, and his family still considers me a part of their family. During these grueling six years my oldest daughter went on to college, and my two other daughters left home, beginning lives of their own.

Letting Go

It used to be children left home
when becoming adults.
Now they sprout their wings and fly
Before knowing it's not nice to pout.
Mom and Dad left to cry
Feeling as if they could die.
Their children gone, they're all alone
Is this how God felt when we left home?
Children now building homes of their own
Some with sand, some with stone.
Raising their children,
As their parents have done
Hopefully training them
For leaving home.

Teri Gambill
August 31, 2000

Looking back, I asked myself, "If I had to do this over again would I change anything?" YES! YES! YES!

I would have taken my daughters and gotten a divorce from the beginning. I would not have put them through the mental anguish it took to *maybe* become a family once more. There are no guarantees in life.

I no longer believe that love is enough. The illusion of having a husband who loves you is not more important than loving yourself or taking care of yourself. Life itself is not a romance, nor is it a fairy tale.

Food for Thought

- As women, we have a built-in, nurturing nature which gives us the motivation and need to make all areas of our lives work. Ex: mothering, marriage, parenting, and our jobs. This gives us the *illusion* that our value rests on the outcome of each segment of our life. Along with this comes the teaching that love, forgiveness, and Jesus Christ go hand-in-hand. With these, everything can be worked out. They, together, endure **all** things.

- We then take personally the responsibility for each outcome, whether the responsibility is ours or not. We will do anything and everything within our power to not hear the words, "I told you so!" or our mothers' famous last words—"You made your bed, now you lie in it!"

- During a relationship it becomes more important to have a significant other who loves us than it is to love ourselves.

- The words broken trust, betrayal, devastation, and sorrow do not even come close to describing the true, deep emotions or feelings we experience when going through *any* of these things. It is a feeling that only those who have experienced them firsthand can understand. Giving us the feeling of being stripped of everything that makes us who we are and leaving us with NOTHING!

- To heal, we learn to take life one minute at a time because this is all we are capable of until such a time when we can handle a little more and a little more after that. The memories are always going to be there. But time has a way of healing the hurt. At said time, we begin to get stronger every day. There is no way to overcome hurt without becoming a stronger person because we all need to face our fears (life) at one point or another to heal and be able to move on.

- A failed marriage, along with children who choose to journey on their own early in life, does not mean we are a failure; it means we need to look at them as a lesson. What can we learn from it all. Ex: accept ourselves for who we are, stay true to ourselves. and continue to do what is right no matter what the circumstances may be.
- We each have a right to make our own mistakes, for this is what life is all about, and judgements should be reserved for God above.
- When we criticize ourselves or others, we are criticizing God!

LESSONS LEARNED

After ending my marriage, I decided to evaluate the path I had taken. What I learned from each trial was to be and strive to be the best I could be. I became aware that there were others who had life a whole lot worse than me. I was the only one who could do anything about **my** life. It was time to move on, and I did not want to repeat the same mistakes I had already made.

One thing I learned when becoming a counselor was "life is sweet when you KISS it." KISS stands for *"keep it simple, silly."* I learned to apply this to myself. I started refusing to get caught up in the chaos of life's negativity (judgements). By doing this, I was taking care of myself. I was determined to learn from my mistakes as well as from the experiences life had handed me thus far. Lessons learned:

- God comes first. When I try to control my life, life goes to hell in a handbasket.
- Life handed me these lessons because of the choices I had made on my life's journey.
- God is too important to be ignored or left behind.
- God does not always give me everything I ask for because, in the long run, it is not in my best interest.
- To be thankful for the blessings I **do have.**
- God does not make junk. God loves me just the way I am. He loves

us all—unconditionally.

- To listen to my intuition. God gave me intuition for a reason.
- When my heart and mind come together, I know it is the right thing to do. Only when this happens do things feel right.
- *Everything* happens for a reason. The reason is not for me to understand.
- Make sure that when I decide on something or make a choice, be it big or small, my intentions and motives are in right perspective.
- To be forgiving. It sets us free to move forward in life without carrying unneeded baggage.
- Without boundaries, we are more focused on others and rarely concerned about what is good for ourselves.
- To turn negatives into positives, no matter what they are. Yes, it's doable!
- To take life one day at a time and to keep it simple.
- At times it is okay to get angry at God, He understands!
- Fairy tale lives and romance do not exist in real life.

When looking back at the churches I had experienced while growing up, I found these commonalities:

- They believed in God and Jesus Christ.
- All believed that you cannot get to God without going through Jesus Christ first. He is the Savior and Lord. The point being that we are all sinners, as human beings.
- We are to rely on God and His promises.
- Those that believe this *fear* God.

This was confusing for me in my younger years. Everyone claimed their church to be "the Church" and yet basically believing much the same way. Whatever I felt in my heart to be good or true, I adopted to my beliefs.

I also knew when I asked for help and surrendered to His will (not mine) and meant it, I received. Maybe **not** in a way **I thought I needed** to receive, but I **did** receive what was best for me. So, I accepted what I had received without question.

After looking at the lessons I had learned and the experiences I had encountered, I reevaluated *my* true beliefs.

My conclusions were…

I believed God **knew** what was in my heart, **heard** anything I said or **thought** anywhere, anytime! He could **see** everything I did, including in the bedroom. I believed that I did not have to be sitting in church just for this to happen.

Jesus administered to people wherever they were. If they came to Him and asked from the heart He save them, He would, even if it was in the middle of the street. He gave them His salvation, anywhere they were.

Also, I believed that my business with God was **between myself and God**, only.

I knew He loved me for who I was; that He made me a unique person. It did not matter what I was wearing, be it jeans and a ratty t-shirt or a dress, or if I was wearing nothing at all. The bathroom is sometimes the only place you can receive any privacy.

I did not have a fear of God either, a great respect yes, fear no. Many times, He is portrayed in the Bible as a loving and forgiving God. Also, the word of God states that He wants us to be loving and forgiving. To back this up, the Golden Rule states, "Do unto others as you would want them to do to you." Why would He be any different? He continuously stands for forgiveness.

REFLECTIONS EXERCISE

- Have you ever thought about your faith?
- Do you know your true spiritual beliefs?
- Do you practice them?
- When has your faith helped you?

CHAPTER 4
A New Beginning

In making the decision to move on with my life and be the best I could be. I decided to expand my horizons and relocate to Washington State.

I was on my own for the very first time in my life; I knew no one. I received a job working as a counselor trainee once again, taking a job in an outpatient treatment center, which I had never done. Again, my Higher Power (God) provided the way.

The importance of self-awareness became obvious to me, as I was teaching the self-awareness group, which was part of my job. *My clients weren't the only ones learning.*

I was thinking of going back to school to get my degree in Human Services, as well as doing work with Good Samaritan Ministries. I had previously received a year of counselor training with them, and I discovered there to be a big difference between alcohol and drug counseling and life coaching, which I felt called to do.

Shortly after realizing the differences in counseling and thinking of going back to school, the center I was working for soon ran out of funding and had to close its doors. Which meant I was no longer employed.

I relocated once more, returning to Oregon. I moved in with a friend, keeping house and preparing meals in return for room and board. It was strictly a roommate situation. Mike believed I could do anything if I put my mind to it. I wanted to go back to school, but the funds were not available.

Months later, my relationship with Mike started to change. We found we really enjoyed each other's company, and we had much in common. We both agreed that we would never marry. We had been there, done that, not again. He taught me to stand up for myself as well as for my beliefs. He made it very clear that any kind of disrespect toward anything or from anybody would not be tolerated.

He, being of Native American descent and having experience within their culture, taught me a little about their traditions and beliefs, bringing us even closer together.

I discovered myself to be what they call an earth person. A person who has the courage to follow the guidance of the heart. A person who resects Native American people, culture, and land. I found myself to be a kindred spirit, believing that everything on earth has a purpose. Believing in the connection between God and all that He created.

As you can see, my beliefs changed once more. Bottom line, for me, there is only one loving God no matter what we call Him, be it Great Spirit, God, Father God, or Higher Power, depending on where you are spiritually. Also, it is our own choice. He is the same God!

Chapter 5
God-Given Tools

Before Mike's job took us to Colorado I was introduced to Reiki, an ancient art of healing originally used by the Tibetan monks, more than twenty-five hundred years ago. Reiki is a Japanese word meaning Spirit (Rei), Energy (ki). It refers to life and substance. All cultures have a name for this energy. Christians use the term Holy Spirit, Hindus use the term Prana, Kahunas use the term Mana, etc. Reiki always serves the individuals highest good; no matter how small, it always heals. Reiki serves all who have an interest in being healthy and balanced. In the philosophy of Reiki, all disease, illness, and discomfort originate from a state of imbalance. This imbalance may occur mentally, physically, or emotionally. For more information concerning Reiki, contact a Reiki Master of the Usui Lineage. My Reiki Master is one of the most beautiful people I know. She is also a very dear friend.

Mike and I were married and moved to Texas for two years. While there, I took the opportunity to learn about metaphysical healing techniques. Such as the healing attributes of crystals, gemstones, and rocks, which contain life force energy as well. Along with the ancient use of herbs, instead of using chemicals. This enabled me to enjoy growing, harvesting, and using my own garden.

Also, while in Texas, Mike succumbed to his calling as a Native American shaman. He began once again to practice the Native shamanism trainings he had once practiced. In so doing, I was introduced to shamanism as well. I had known he had healing abilities but never suspected how advanced he truly was.

There are many culturally different shamans. Mike instructed me in the ways of a Comanche shaman. A true shaman believes everything (be it a rock, water, fire, air, trees, plants, stars, the moon and sun), no matter what size, is alive and possesses a spirit.

They gain their knowledge from other shamans as well as the Spirits—mostly the Spirits. It is not something that can be learned overnight, during a weekend, or over a couple of months. It takes years of practice and work under the guidance of a shaman to fully understand the energies in all living things. Shamanism is very involved and can be very intense at times.

True shamans do not seek to control or seek to feel important in any way; they shed the ego completely; they genuinely give of their services, be it guidance, healing, or wisdom when called upon.

A gift of thanks, something created from the heart, something you highly treasure, tobacco, or sage is given to the shaman for his services.

Not everybody who claims to be a shaman is one. If you seek the help of a shaman, it is strongly advised that you check credentials. Asking how long they have studied, with whom and where? Choosing a shaman is like choosing the very best doctor in the country.

Another tool God has supplied me with is the Animal Medicine oracle cards. I receive my answers from them quite often. Sometimes, I need an extra incentive or confirmation that I am on the right track. I still doubt myself at times, and this keeps me focused. My personal opinion regarding tarot cards and/or oracle cards is they should be used for spiritual reasons only. Spirituality, connecting with God, receiving guidance from God are what they were created for, nothing else, *especially not fortune telling*. Otherwise, you're messing around with God's plan. This I do not agree with. When the cards are used with the wrong intentions, the ego is involved, leaving no room for the presence of spirituality.

We have many God-given tools available to us. All we need to do is be willing to learn about them and ask if they could help us along our path in any way and apply them to our own style. They were provided for a reason. I am not saying any of them are the *only* right way to God. I only know what works for me; what gave me hope when I needed it most. It has been different tools, i.e., Christianity, Reiki, or medicine cards at different times in my life. The one thing I do know is that there is always an alternative to every situation. We just need to be **willing** to find it. Be open-minded as well as open-hearted. To take that first step in changing/learning whatever life lesson we are going through at the time. *Only we can do this for ourselves; no one else can do it for us.*

REFLECTIONS EXERCISE:

- What God-given tool have you discovered, and how has it helped you?
- What might you be interested in as an alternative?

Food for Thought

- How many of us stay with tradition even though it is not working for us?
- Why do we have to follow tradition instead of finding what personally works for us?

Going South

Choices and options have been discerned
Life lessons yet to be learned
A new start we have yearned
Home to Texas we came
finding nothing the same
Have our efforts been in vain?
Knowing trials were to come
A team, we've become
Standing now as one
With confidence being gained
The sky we have aimed
A united team we've became

Teri Prock
July 7, 2004

CHAPTER 6
Lessons in Self-Awareness/
Self Preservation

Hindsight showed me that we should never have moved to Texas. However, many good things resulted from this move. Mike and I received an attitude adjustment, along with finding and living our spirituality.

Before going to Texas, I felt called "by the Holy Spirit" to lead groups when we were all settled in. They were to be self-awareness groups given on a donation basis. I didn't follow my intuition concerning these groups; I doubted my capabilities. I did not have a college education for this. Therefore, I resisted the idea of leading said groups. The only credentials I had were my life experiences along with what I had learned by being a counselor. I preferred *life coach* instead of *counselor*. It does not scare people or give them the impression that I want to mess with their mind.

Sometimes people just need a sound board to make their own decisions.

Nine months later, after receiving many hints concerning said groups and ignoring them, I got another wake-up call. God had my attention once more. It does not pay to ignore the Holy Spirit.

After surrendering to the Holy spirit, I started the groups on self-awareness. I started with just three women, counting myself. The lessons and associated materials were presented to me in a dream. After writing the instructions down, I remember thinking, "How phenomenal!" I never dreamed that being a vessel for God could increase one's knowledge in such a remarkable way. Our first lesson was on perceiving. Here is how it went:

EXERCISE

- If you could be a tree, what kind would it be?
- Have each member draw and color their tree.
- Write why you would be said tree.
- How would you spread your joy?
- How could you help others?
- What kind of people would you attract?
- Describe what kind of nourishment your tree would receive right now, this moment!
- Compare yourself to the tree you just drew and described. Are they the same?
- Ask for group feedback concerning each tree drawn.

Each one of us sees, hears, and perceives things differently. Be it our surroundings or words and the tone of voice used. Ex: How many people do you know perceive their childhood the very same way as their parents do? Each person's perception is very real to them. There is no right or wrong. They are just different.

You ask how this fits with *Faith as an Alternative?* Everyone observes worship, prayer, faith, and spirituality in various ways, along with how you should pray or not pray, what words should be used, and how they should be spoken. Everyone's relationship with God varies; perceiving also ties in with the Bible. This is where the tree exercise coincides with the Bible in Luke 6:43, 44: *No good tree bears bad fruit, nor does a bad tree bear good fruit. Each tree is recognized by its own fruit.* People do not pick figs from thorn bushes, or grapes from briars.

When we hang on to the past and the negatives (judgements) it contains, our tree (meaning us as individuals) is blocked from the channel of nourishment. When our spirit is malnourished, we are incapable of nourishing others properly as well. It also puts a barrier between us and our God-given foundation. It closes us off from the Christ consciousness. How can we rightly perceive if we are closed off? Everyone's truth is different. How can we know the truth about anyone besides ourselves, since we cannot see through God's eyes to see what His plans are for each and every one of us? We need to take a good look at ourselves first before we try to help others. Our own lives are unique from anyone else's. How others see us may very well be contrary to how we see ourselves, and that is okay!

After our first group, it was decided that we should expand and become co-ed. My house was not big enough, and to make an accommodation for this, a small church offered their building. A small factor here: the church consisted of agnostics, atheists, and many different denominations. We had a great response and a few members of the church attended as well.

I asked God, "Is this really where you want me?" A few days later I was asked to speak at a Sunday meeting. I had never spoken to a congregation before. Once again, what were my qualifications? The message I received via this small voice in my ear was, "Who needs qualifications to deliver a message!" The information for the message I was to deliver came to me once more through a dream. I was to speak on "how negativity can affect us"! The message and exercise were all there. I questioned God once more, "God, are you sure this is what you want delivered?" I received confirmation, and I delivered said message, with good responses from all who attended. Why? Because I went about it the way God had led me to.

The exercise went as follows (try this for yourself):

- Take a sheet of paper and fold it in thirds.
- Write on the top third, *How has my negativity affected others and who has it affected?*
- Write on the middle third, *How has others' negativity affected me?*
- On the bottom third, take each negative and turn it into a positive
- Where would you be today if you had taken positive action instead?

We all encounter some form of negativity daily; it's not only in our personal lives. It is in our jobs, schools, society, the news, politics, and even some churches. Remember, it is what we decide to do with negativity that matters.

While examining negativity we felt a need a need to look at boundaries. The definition of boundaries: that which you are or are not willing to experience, be it socially, emotionally, physically, sexually, or spiritually.

Our boundaries influence the amount of negativity that we entail daily. They also affect the way we make or do not make decisions! Boundaries define who we truly are. When setting clear precise boundaries, we take responsibility for our own lives, which, in turn, gives us many different options as to what, where, when, or how we can *choose* to experience anything.

Without boundaries, our options are very limited. *Without them we let everyone else choose for us* what they want us to experience. Ex: We become a doormat for those around us; we say "yes" when we would like to say "no"; we get taken for granted. Meaning, we let people disrespect us.

With clearly defined boundaries we know where our rights end and another person's rights begin. A good way to keep our boundaries in perspective is to ask ourselves these questions:

- Is this my problem?
- Is this someone else's problem?
- Is this something I *can* change or do anything about?
- Is it *my* responsibility, or does the responsibility belong to *someone else*?

We are the only ones who can teach others how to treat us. People will not know how to treat us if we don't tell them. We can't *blame* anybody for mistreating us if we do not tell them, "*It is not okay!*" This also goes with responsibility. Put responsibility where it belongs. We *are not responsible* for anyone's decisions, choices, actions, reactions, or responsibilities **but our own**! Our boundaries consist of our taking responsibility for what concerns us, not everybody else.

Using the animal kingdom as an example, animals respect each other's turf (boundaries). Their boundaries are not wishy-washy but consistent.

They have ways of peacefully communicating them and making them stick. They each give the appropriate space to live peacefully and for the good of the whole.

Again, I received through a dream another important lesson: decisions. This one, as it happened, turned out to be the favorite.

The word decisions is a static word. Decisions are like a staircase. They are the steps we take that enable us to learn the life lessons given us to reach our destination.

The exercise went like this (again, try this for yourself):

- On a piece of paper draw your personal staircase.
- While looking at it, ask these questions:
- Is your staircase rickety? Full of doubt, negativity, not able to climb forward, upward? Is it weak? What supports it?
- Is it unstable? Some of everything, wishy-washy, a little doubt, maybe missing a few steps, wobbly, deteriorating not much confidence. What is it based on?
- Is it solid? Built with a good foundation, confidence, positive inner knowing, consistency. Will it meet your goals?

Respect

The word choices is positive. Leaving no room for doubt. I prefer choices! As we get better at making choices, our staircase grows taller and stronger one step at a time, gently rising. We would not be the people we are today without the trials of life. They are what make us strong. Independent people with courage to move on in life. To be the best that we can possibly be, if we choose to do so. It does not mean we are weak if we need a little extra help from a Higher Power. Everything happens for a reason! Romans 5:3, 4, 5: *Tribulations bring about perseverance and perseverance yields a crop of character.*

It helps to look at our trials and tribulations as life-learning lessons. Then take said lessons and become *willing, honest, and open minded* to look at the part we *truly* played in them. As well as being willing to accept the answers.

When we are close minded, we tend to take the easy way out change the things we can. Without this honesty and courage, we would continue exactly as we are.

If we choose to do nothing and tell ourselves "I cannot do this" or "I cannot do that," we never will! Therefore, indirectly, we are saying, "I would rather be a doormat and live a life filled with doubt, insecurities, drama, and chaos." When we choose to follow the road of resistance, we are in no way allowing ourselves to be open-hearted or open-minded.

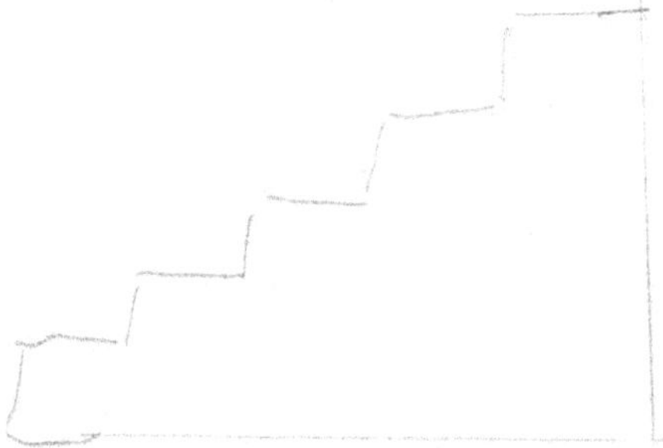

What does your personal foundation look like?

We need to examine our intentions, the reason for doing the things we do. Are we seeking approval, maybe trying to please everybody else but ourselves or do we have a fear of rejection? Only we can answer these questions for ourselves. Now it is up to us to do something positive about it.

Living a life such as this causes blockages in our soul, not allowing the Holy Spirit to communicate with us. Where, as if, we were to be open-hearted and open-minded, we would be receptive to a Higher Power. Know that it **is within you** to make a difference in your life. Faith can be a wonderful alternative for not taking the road of negativism.

Let me ask you this, how wide are your shoulders? How wide do you think God's are? What could it hurt to hand over your trials and tribulations to God or a Higher Power? I would like to share a piece I found in the *Women's Devotional Bible* by Brenda Wilbee that puts things in a unique perspective:

Tell me, did Cinderella live happily ever after without a struggle? Did Sleeping Beauty live happily ever after without trauma? Did Rapunzel live happily ever after without grief? Did Hansel and Gretel live happily ever after without deprivation? Did Jack and the Beanstalk live happily ever after without risk? Did Thumbelina live happily ever after without sacrifice? Are there any fairy tales without any dragons? Where in the world, then did we ever get the notion that to live happily ever after means to live without trouble? For when we look at fairy tales we find it's not the absence of dragons – but the taming of the dragons – that ushers in happily ever after.

REFLECTIONS EXERCISE

- Do you want to continue a life filled with negativity, i.e., irresponsibility, chaos, drama?
- Are you being honest with yourself?
- What are your intentions?
- Are you being open or close minded?

When we are close minded, we put the blame on others, wallowing in self-pity, thus sharing no responsibility for anything. Therefore, stagnating us in a plaguing situation, which then robs us of our true potential, blinding us from seeing the opportunities that God does provide.

Being open-minded and honest is a necessity when looking at our alternatives. It enables us to find courage too.

One of the first steps out of negativism is gratitude. Counting the blessings you do have. *Women's Devotional Bible*, 1 Timothy 4:4: *For everything God created is good and nothing is to be rejected if it is received with thanksgiving.* Just being alive is a blessing. Looking at life from a positive point of view is like looking at night and day. For instance, the lesson our group did on gratitude. Everyone received hope, that little light at the end of the tunnel. Life is not so bad when we are focused on the positives. It went as follows (you try it too!):

Gratitude Exercise:

- Write down what gratitude means to you!
- Make a list of the things you are grateful for.
- When was the last time you made a list of the things you are grateful for?
- Did it include all or any of your trials and tribulations? Why or why not?
- Take a sheet of paper and down the left side spell out gratitude.
- For each letter starting with G, write positive words that apply to you and your life. Ex: G = goodness, grateful, grace, R = respectful, righteous.

Gratitude should be recognized daily. It keeps us *focused* and gives us that little bit of *hope* that many of us have lost along the way. As well as keeping us focused it gives us the courage to step up and say, "I am a good person, and I can and will change that which needs changing." It also brings us a new sense of self. We become a person who is aware of our attitudes and beliefs. Along with the knowledge that we have become more flexible in life, handling each life experience that comes our way, knowing also that we will become a stronger person with each life lesson. It in turn gives us a sense of accomplishment.

When we are in a thankful frame of mind, we are being simple minded, meaning abstaining from chaos. Most of us think of simple and positive things to be grateful for. Ex: a rood over our head, food, and clothes. Never once including our trials. The longer we are in a positive frame of mind, the easier it becomes to be thankful for the trials and tribulations as well.

When we are not in a thankful frame of mind, life is hard. We make it harder than it needs to be because of our attitudes. When we focus on our chaotic lives, we must know why this, why that, why me, what next? A chaotic life makes living much more difficult.

You say, "I have talked to God and He ignored me. It's like He isn't even there." *We must meet Him halfway. God is not going to do all the work for us!* Like the old saying you heard in school about how they supplied us with books and more books, and we "didn't" learn anything. Why? Because we did not read them. Also, we need a positive change in attitude, and it needs to *stay changed.* Our answers will come in His timing not ours.

CHAPTER 7
The KISS of Life

Reflecting on the "KISS of Life," life is so much sweeter when you KISS it. "Keep it simple, silly." Here is an example of being simple minded:

When we get into a car to go somewhere, we just do it. Giving no thought to whether it might fall apart while driving down the road. Nor do we question each time whether we will be in an accident. We just get in and drive, knowing they will take us where we need to go, and we will get there. Never doubting anything about it. No worries, no chaos, no drama. Just doing and knowing.

This next example shows the simplicity of prayer. Eliminating the fear of whether you are praying correctly or not, along with squelching any doubts that you may have as to whether He is with you or not.

When we ask God more than one time for anything, we are assuming that He has not already done it, "doubting Him." When we ask God to be with us for whatever reason, we are assuming that He is not *already there, "doubting His presence."* When we call His attention to our impatience, "Are you listening to me?" "Today would be sufficient!" or "Anytime would be nice you know!" because we have doubted Him once again, His response could be "It will be another day in coming too!" Patience is a virtue, and a virtue never hurt you!

When we thank God for anything, there is no doubt. When we thank Him for being with us and keeping us safe, there is no doubt. Talking to God as if He were our best friend eliminates all the religious control of having to

65

pray a certain way for everything and anything. The only thing we need to remember is that prayers are answered in His timing. He knows what is in our best interests because He sees our future we do not.

When keeping life simple, it enables us to enjoy more of life. Simplicity supplies us with laughter and fun. Why? Because we are not caught up in the family drama or the chaotic negativism (judgements) of life. We have chosen to stay involved with only that which involves us directly. We have chosen not to worry about the small stuff! We know also that we do not have to take on others' problems to be a good friend. That is God's job!

Learning to laugh at life's situations is a big key to staying out of chaos, stress, or drama. Humor takes the edge off stressful situations, as most of us know. Finding humor in each day provides us with a laugh a day. Doc Prock's theory: "A laugh a day keeps the doctor away!"

Chapter 8
Key Elements

As we established much earlier, we arrive here on earth as our true-self, innocent, happy, forgiving, and willing to love.

We reviewed a few God-given tools, along with several self-awareness/self-preservation techniques. By taking part in the exercises, we found within ourselves a desire to improve our life as well as ourselves.

In reviewing said tools, we found faith to be an alternative and learned that God has provided many tools, for us. Along with this we looked at the following:

- *Perceiving* – No one sees, hears, or speaks *exactly* like another individual.
- *Boundaries* – Without them, everyone else *but us* decides what we should be doing and how we should be doing it.
- *Negativity* – Chaos, dysfunction, stress, we are all much better off without it.
- *Gratitude* – Enables us to *put things* in right perspective.
- *KISS* – Keep It Simple, Silly (The Kiss of Life). This enables us to keep all of the above in the right perspective.

Along with the above, we learned that we are enrolled in a school called life. While attending this school of life we have had all kinds of garbage (negatives) thrown at us, and to our misfortune it has stuck to us like glue. It can be gotten rid of, yes, but it is not easy. Most of it has permeated deep within, causing considerable damage emotionally, socially, and spiritually. Getting rid of this trash requires us to go dumpster diving (sorting out the trash), keeping the good (truth) and discarding the bad (lies).

For us to apply our God-given tools and the self-preservation techniques, we need to take an *honest* look at our *own view* of our *own* self-worth and self-esteem. These being the two most important things for self-preservation.

When we apply everything we have learned with good self-worth and good self-esteem, it enables us to feel complete (whole), feeling good about *ourselves* and *life* in general. Most importantly, *accepting ourselves for who we truly are*, a good, worthy, and loving person striving to be the best we can be, and along with God's help, be in charge or our own life instead of having someone else control us.

Knowing that making changes within ourselves is not an easy task. Are we ready to sort through the trash and get honest with ourselves, to once again become our real and true self?

Circle One: Yes or No

If not, put this book down and do not read any further. Please know that my prayers are with you and I wish you the best.

If you think you can do a thing,
Or think you can't do a thing you're right.
Henry Ford

I am delighted you decided to join us! Choosing to get honest and take responsibility for ourselves to make appropriate changes says, "I want a better life for myself; only the truth can set me free!"

In the end, I vow that those of us who are truly honest will have within themselves the strength, courage, and confidence to ensure an awesome, new lifestyle.

Remember, it will not be easy. Although it is necessary to take control of our own life as well as *knowing* the truth and not accepting the lies or the illusions we have come to believe or that others would like us to believe.

You gain strength, courage, and confidence
By every experience in which you really
Stop to look fear in the face.
Eleanor Roosevelt

CHAPTER 9
Truths

First let's examine the word self-worth according to a few dictionaries:

New World Dictionary: Self – 1. The identity, character, or essential qualities of any person. 2. Anything considered as having a distinct personality.

Webster's Dictionary: Worth – 1. Value or excellence of any kind. 2. The quality or combination of qualities that makes one deserving of esteem.

Quality as defined by Webster's dictionary:

> Quality – 1. The basic essential character nature, etc. of something 2. Excellence; quality rather than quantity. 3. The degree of excellence. 4. Amoral or personality trait or characteristic.

> Summarized – The value we place on the qualities that make us our own distinct self. In short, the value we give ourselves, what we believe about ourselves. Respecting oneself.

When God created all, He designed His creations for *quality*, not *worthlessness. We were created as quality human beings, and the creator trusted us to treat ourselves as such.*

Regarding self-worth, let's go back to the day we arrived here on earth. God instilled within each and every one of us a combination of essential quality seeds. This combination consisted of seeds of goodness, forgiveness, happiness, a willingness to love unconditionally, innocence; seeds of faith (trust), hope; seeds of character, discipline (self-control), confidence, courage, endurance, patience, and contentment. All of which require much TLC (tender loving care), nurturing, and guidance to fully blossom within us.

Most of us love a beautiful flower garden and take much pride in a thriving vegetable garden, but we neglect to feel or treat ourselves and others the same way.

Only with proper care may the quality seeds within our garden (ourselves) flourish and reach their full potential. If our seeds are cut off in any way from the nourishment needed, we struggle throughout life. In comparing our garden (ourselves) to that of a vegetable garden, we will find the following:

Using these abbreviations:

N = nurturing, guidance, TLC
M = Mistreated, abused

RADISH

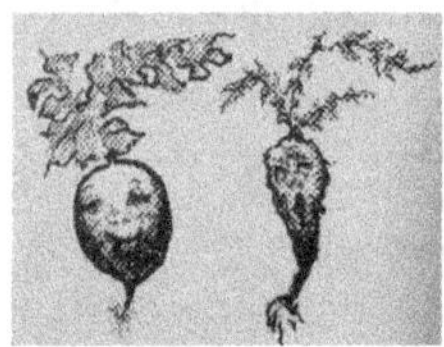

N = nicely rounded, juicy, crisp, contained pizazz (self-control)
M = get very hot and sassy if they don't get enough water (discipline) to cool their jets

TURNIP

N = nice-sized, juicy, with rounded amount of starch (confidence) to face anything and survive
M = small, soft (no confidence)

Carrots

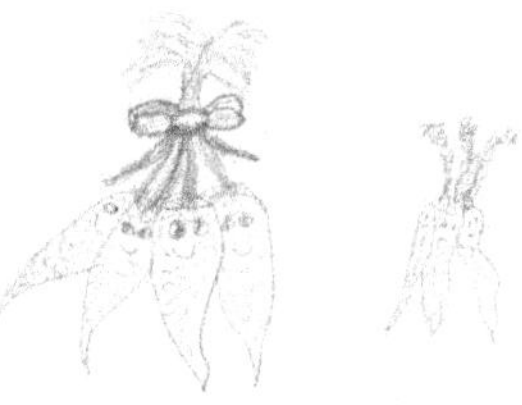

N = rich in color, good size, containing courage to face adversity continuing to grow till late fall
M = small, dull, bland (no courage)

Peas

N = are content to stay within their means, remaining tasty, plump, and sweet
M = wither up, become unfruitful and die

Spinach

N = iron enriched, with nice firm leaves
M = wilted, not enough strength to go on

When we choose to treat ourselves as worthless, choose to listen to others and do nothing, **we are choosing to believe the illusions that others would want us to believe.** Let me point out there is nothing in the definition of self-worth or quality that says anything about our behavior, our looks, or others' opinions.

Our definitions would not be complete if we did not examine the final and most recognized definition of self-worth. This definition has been carried to extremes and passed down from generation to generation. The definition is that of society.

In society our self-worth is based on our performances and others' opinions. This could not be more wrong! **In reality** our self-worth consists of **true facts** about us and **facts only.**

So, it is here we get into dumpster diving (sorting through the trash). Separating the facts from the lies.

Dive #1. Our self-worth is not in our ancestry, it is not in the color of our skin, nor is it in what we have.

Society, television, big-time movies, commercials, magazines, school, and peers all tell us that we can have, have, and have more *if…*

So, we naturally conclude that the way to be happy and feel good about ourselves is through what we have or in fulfilling the *ifs*. Examples: diet pills etc. For the traditional ten-figure, new home of our own, a jet ski, new car, four-wheelers, brand-name clothes and household items. **THIS IS A LIE!** When what we have is never enough, we can be sure that we have bought the lie of IF ONLY I HAD… Monetary things make us feel better for a time, but soon we find another if to fulfill because we continue to place absolutely no value on ourselves, leaving the same void to occur over and over and over. Self-worth is not in what we have but in who we truly are!

Dive #2. Our worth is not in what we do!

Let me introduce you to the do-over game. It can come from childhood, emotionally abusive relationships, even some jobs. It is caused by a voice that repeatedly says to us, "You can do better," "That wasn't good enough," or "I'm not good enough." This in turn drives us to get so involved and extremely committed to everything and anything, meanwhile doing nothing for ourselves. Therefore, we believe in the illusion that our worth is in what we do. Over and over and over.

Dive #3. Our self-worth is not in what we know!

Our world (society) is constantly changing, and the need for education has become extremely important. In turn, many of us have begun to feel "less than" (inadequate), causing many of us to strive for more and more knowledge, thinking when we get that college degree, we will have reached our goal. The truth being we continue to strive for "being adequate."

How many of us have degrees today? What was our motive in the beginning?

We tend to forget our skills, what we do know, and the talents we do have. The knowledge gained by our experiences is the highest education we can receive.

Many years ago, I had a hang up! I truly believed I could not possibly be a good counselor because I had no college degree. I was informed that my experiences accounted for more than a college degree. That a person can read book after book and never really know the extent of compassion, empathy, and common sense needed to help people. I then was hired as a counselor trainee and obtained on-the-job training, more experience.

Our worth is in who we are; we do not have to know more than that. The best contribution we can make to this world is the gift of ourselves, knowing and appreciating ourselves for who we are. Self-worth is one of the most important things we will ever master.

We need to learn to enjoy being ourselves, enjoy our own talents and skills. Our self-worth is in who we are. The best we know we can be!

Dive #4. Our self-worth is not in our physical appearance!

Again, society has played a major role. Society has been judging people by their looks for centuries. How many of us realize that 90 percent of the people who are actors, actresses, models, CEOs of big companies, just to mention a few, have paid extensively for their looks with personal trainers, diets, makeup, and/or surgeries. Again, it is who we are inside that is most important!

I was working in a truck stop coffee shop one time and a trucker had stopped for fuel and coffee. The front desk clerks saw him and ran to the break room (which was in the center between the fuel side and the coffee bar), motioning for me to leave my position and get to the break room quickly. Mind you, they had chosen not to wait on him and disappeared instead. Before I knew it, he had come around the corner for coffee. I then found out what the commotion was all about! My first thought was "Oh my gosh! It is Satan Himself!" This man had been tattooed all over, his eyelids, and there were triangles tattooed above and below his eyes. His lips, ears, his face (had whiskers). One arm had satanic tattoos, the other had Christian. My thoughts were very negative, but I heard this voice in my ear saying, "Judge not lest you be judged in like manner." I quietly said to that voice, "You're right." I plastered the biggest genuine smile on my face and cheerfully asked him, "How ya doin' today?"

He responded with a big smile and said, "I'll get my coffee here, but not my fuel! Your fuel attendants are very judgmental. I haven't had any coffee for at least a hundred seventy-five miles due to people's judgements." He thanked me for my attitude, said he would be right back, that he needed to retrieve his thermoses. He brought in seven large thermoses to be filled with coffee. We then we started visiting, and he admitted that he had done some things in life he was not proud of and had many regrets, but it was a little late. He confided that he had become a born-again Christian and found the woman of his dreams. That they had six beautiful children! We had a wonderful visit, and I have to say that he taught me the true meaning of "don't judge a book by its cover," and I would like to thank him for it. If I had not listened to that small, still voice I would have missed a wonderful opportunity and a very important lesson from God!

Weight has become a major part of society as well. Whether we have an abundance of or a lack of. But does a person's weight tell anything about their personality or what's inside their heart? Does the *public really know* all there is to know about *everyone's* personal health? NO! Furthermore, what we weigh, what we look like, or how we got our looks is no one's business but our own. Our ancestors, along with our father and mother, determined our build and what we would naturally look like. The choice was not up to us!

Who we are again depends on what is inside. What will take us farthest in life? Our weight, our looks, or our heart (character traits)?

Dive #5. Our worth is not in what other people think!

Our creator gave each of us a brain, and in this brain, He installed an ability to think for ourselves. Within these thoughts, we hold the power to draw our own conclusions concerning **us**! These conclusions give us the power to make our own choices (what we believe or do not believe, what we need or don't need, what we know, or don't want to know, what we have or don't have, what we do or do not do, what we want to look like or do not want to look like), and not let everyone else make those choices for us. In separating our thoughts and conclusions from those of others, it enables us to become our own individual, our own unique self. Therefore, we do not have to listen to others' sarcasm, cynical remarks, or put downs.

Imagine what the world would be like if we were all joined by the brain. What a confusing, jumbled-up mess we would be. To accomplish anything, we would have to become one giant clone, thinking alike, acting alike, and being alike so we could just function. There would be no individuality. NONE! If God had wanted only one personality, only unit of thought, He would have done in the beginning. When we believe the illusion (lie) that our self-worth lies outside our self, we are being dependent on others for our happiness and the warm and loving feelings toward ourselves. How miserable!

When we were babies, did we care whether we had any clothes on or if we had Nike shoes? How do you think we felt about our skin, whether we had our face on or not, or how we were built? Did we worry about what our life was like, what people thought of us? **NO!** The reality is it never occurred to us. Why? Because we were already important and loved. The things that were important to us were food, being dry, and being warm. We were happy. What we did not tolerate was not having our needs met and people who did not have our best interests at heart. Surprise! Our boundaries were established way back when. If we did not tolerate certain things or behaviors in the beginning, why are we now? At that time, we were happy just being *ourselves*! We are the same person today as we were then, just older!

We **are** *quality human beings*. Our worth lies within the seeds of goodness that God provided us with, the **true facts** of our hearts. All that is needed is to nurture and nourish them.

SELF-ESTEEM

What exactly is self-esteem? According to the New World Dictionary, it is belief in oneself; self-respect.

We discovered ourselves to have been born as human beings, with quality seeds of goodness, character, faith, and hope. Our journey through life may not have nourished these seeds, but they are there. It is up to us to bring them to fruition.

With this said, it is time to believe in ourselves and start treating ourselves with the respect we deserve. Most of us are slow to do this because we keep reliving the past and are saying things like, "Yeah, but there is some truth to what people are saying" or "But I don't deserve it." Okay! Maybe we haven't been perfect. There may be a few misdeeds or even infractions in our past, but this does not mean we have to suffer or pay for them throughout the rest of our life.

The sarcastic and cynical things that people think, say, or do to us do not matter. Society and those who like to think they are in charge of our life have abused their right to an opinion by being judgmental. These people are only carrying on tradition—what they have been taught, instead of thinking about what they are saying or doing. It is what **we choose to believe about ourselves that is important.**

A belief my husband shared with me and I found to help me stand up for who I am today goes like this: "If you don't like me for who I am or how I look, you have three other directions from which to choose," along with telling myself, "I can do or be anything I put my mind to" and "I am who I am, and I like me!"

It is one thing to look at our own self-importance and another to look at only our self as important. This is called self-centered, egotistical, and just plain selfish, among other things. Yes! We need to look out for number one. But looking out for number one is taking care of our well-being emotionally, physically, and spiritually, without being selfish, egotistical, or disrespectful.

What we think of ourselves speaks volumes to others as well… It is portrayed in our behavior. If our behavior contains low self-worth or self-esteem, we are projecting, "I don't like or believe in me, so why should you?" Which in turn tells people we do not care how they treat us because when we do not respect ourselves or believe in ourselves, no one else is going to either.

Our negative behavior attracts negative people to us. We attract what we have become. Negative. Therefore, continuously spinning the merry-go-round of negativity.

We need to think enough of ourselves to make a change for the better and stop this wheel of negativity.

We can't love or take care of anyone else (properly) until we can appropriately love and take care of ourselves. By loving and taking care of ourselves, we can comprehend matters in a right perspective. With nothing added or taken away.

When our beliefs about ourselves turn positive, the negatives disappear. Why? Because there is no longer anything to feed off of (our negativity). Making room for more and more good in our lives.

Think about it! Would we be where we are today, as strong as we are, if it were not for the trials and pleasures in our lives? Have we not gone ahead and done what we needed *to, to get through our day? Then when we look back at* them, we wonder, how did we do it? We have the ability to drop our judgments and learn from life.

CHAPTER 10
Moving Forward/Taking Control

Before moving forward, we need to ask this question, "Why do we believe others are smarter than we are when it comes to our own welfare or well-being?" The answer: we lack faith and trust within ourselves and God.

To begin moving forward we need to start with faith and trust. Faith—in ourselves and God; trust—in ourselves and God. For without them, we have nothing to work with. Faith and trust enable us to develop our own individuality; therefore, everyone's truth will be different. What is right for some may not be right for others.

Not many of us were conditioned to think for ourselves, let alone trust in ourselves. While small, we were taught that Mom and Dad knew what was best and right for us and to listen when spoken to. Later we began to listen to our friends, thinking they knew what they were talking about, and it always sounded better than our parents. By this time, we had also become good listeners.

Also, due to conditioning, many of us were raised knowing who God is, but spirituality was non-existent. Therefore, we were not able to combine our spiritual knowledge with spiritual experiences.

When taking control and responsibility for ourselves (so that one may move forward), we need to be prepared because *we will* come across difficult situations and confrontations. This being the reason that thinking and trusting in ourselves is not easy.

When we stand up for ourselves (take control of our own life), refusing to be a doormat, a people pleaser, or a puppet on a string that everyone can play with, certain family members, some friends, and co-workers (just to name a few) will not see these changes for what they truly are (good changes). They will tend to gossip about us, as well as accuse us of not being the person we used to be.

Example: "Sarah has changed! She is not the kind, loving, giving, compassionate person she used to be. She used to be willing to do anything for anybody, anytime. But not now! I think it's that man she's with. Since meeting him she's just not the same!" Sarah is the same person inside, loving, caring, and compassionate. The difference between then and now is that Sarah got a life of her own, set her boundaries, and stuck to them, expecting respect and choosing to do only that which she felt was important or that she wanted to; in short, she did what was right and good for her. She took control of her own life! Truth be told, that man of hers supported her, which in turn gave her confidence (a backbone)!

The people who were involved in this scenario did not see Sarah's changes as good because they did not have control of Sarah's life, nor was she at their beck and call anymore.

Similar situations to this are the main reason most of us revert to the old ways. Why? We start having feelings of betrayal, guilt, and/or shame because we have upset someone, which then turned into everyone. Once again feeling as if everything is our fault, and we are being selfish. To move past these feelings we need to remember we have the right to be in control of ourselves, as well as possessing the power within to stay true to ourselves and become the very best we can possibly be!

You know, God is forgiving, He does allow U-turns, and in doing so He gives us many chances. If He didn't, the world would have ended long ago!

Keeping this in mind helps us to begin our lives anew, by wiping our slates clean, discarding the garbage that comes our way, and striving to be the very best we know and believe we can be.

How do we strive to be the very best we know and believe we can be? By building on our strengths. What strengths, you ask? Remember? We were born with goodness. We just need to nurture that goodness and listen to our own hearts (not others' opinions). To help you on this journey through life is an exercise that can be a mental "note to self," or may I suggest writing it out, so you can compare in three to six months (hence able to keep track of your progress)?

What do our hearts say about us?

EXERCISE:

- Write a paragraph on who you truly are, using your very own heartfelt beliefs concerning yourself. Other opinions not allowed!
- Look at the list of strengths provided on next page and take the following inventory of your strengths by listening to your own heart. Then write the date at the bottom.
- On a different piece of paper take the strengths you checked, add the ones you would like to adopt to your character, and write "I am…" in front of each one. Then place the list where you can see it and read it daily. In one month's time, take the inventory again. Please feel free to add any additional strengths as well. Compare!

LIST OF STRENGTHS

loving	goal-oriented	courageous
honest	organized	happy
capable	team player	attractive
handsome	detail-oriented	brave
faithful	open-minded	supportive
trusting	humorous	content
an encourager	responsible	enthusiastic
forgiving	prompt	cute
lovable	good listener	compassionate
focused	ethical	assertive
accepting	good mother	good father
persistent	ambitious	consistent
cautious	competitive	giving
creative	committed	attractive
confident	self-respectful	kind
disciplined	respectful	self-control
fair		

First Date __________________________________

Second Date________________________________

Now that we have established our strengths, let's review the beginning steps we've taken towards our new life:

1. We found the courage to have faith and trust within ourselves and a Higher Power/God.
2. Realized God does not make junk—we do! God designed us with quality seeds of goodness, faith character, and hope, making us quality human beings.
3. Established that our self-worth lies within ourselves and the person we choose to be. Self-worth has nothing to do with the following:
   a) our skin color,
   b) what we do, or how we do,
   c) what we have,
   d) what we know,
   e) what we look like, and
   f) it's definitely not in other's opinions.
4. Learned that God has given us our own individuality, meaning the ability to think for ourselves, speak for ourselves, draw our own conclusions, make our own choices, and most importantly, the ability to believe in ourselves

5. Found that taking control of our own life sets the stage for self-respecting boundaries and in turn enables us to receive respect as well.
6. When our beliefs about ourselves turn positive, the negatives dis-

appear. Making room for more and more positives.

7. To be thankful for our trials as well as our pleasures because without them we would not be the unique person we are today. Having gratitude.

8. Realized that life's trials will never cease. It is what we choose to do with them that is important.

9. The past is the past. There are no do-overs. However, God grants us many chances. He allows U-turns.

10. Learned that along with seeds of goodness, God supplied us with strengths. That we need to nurture and build on them.

Living with integrity and grace

We may need to review this material to stay focused on our new life's journey, as well as complete the exercises once again to compare to the first. This in turn will confirm our progress.

One really important thing to remember is, once we take control of our lives, it is easy to overstep our boundaries and cross someone else's. Why? Because when we realize that our lives have begun to change for the better, we humans tend to want to fix everyone else's life too. Meaning it's easy to tip the scale and begin trying to control others also.

We can be the person who turns negatives into positives, we can be the example of the person who walks their talk, but the best thing we can do for others is love and accept them for who they are and be an encourager of the good things in life as well as be the example for others to see! By remaining in this positive state (being the best we can be), others will begin changing along with us, due to our example.

Whether a person chooses to participate in life the same as we do is their choice. For others need to learn their own life lessons on the playground of life the same as we did. Remember everyone is an individual, with the ability to choose what's right for them and when!

"I HAVE A RIGHT"

"I have a right" only, says a wise sage, if you accept
The responsibility that goes with it.
We have a right to be full-fledged people of dignity and
Decency and respectful to those around us.
The right for a good life belongs to all of us—as long as
We value it, work for it, and keep it good.
We have a right to speak our minds, but we have to know
The tremendous responsibility of words.
We have a right to cultivate our spiritual preferences and to see them
Bear fruit in every good thing.
It is our right to be who we are without the burden of
Regret and resentment. But we have to remember that our rights are
Limited to where our rights end and another person's rights begin
Plenty Coups 1848
Taken from *A Cherokee Feast of Days Daily Meditations*
Joyce Sequichie

Epilogue

My spiritual beliefs and opinions have been redefined over the past several years. My prior beliefs were believing in a loving and forgiving God, who created and provided all things with a spirit (Life Force Energy); believing Jesus Christ was here on earth and died for our salvation; that God is everywhere, in everything; and my business is between God and myself only. In the past few years, I have gained knowledge and experiences which led me to combine my prior beliefs with the following:

I believe the Bible was true at one time; however, I do not see how it could contain its original meaning after two thousand years of human translations and revisions. Considering our language today, all over the world, consists of words that do not mean the same as they did just twenty years ago, let alone two thousand. Along with this is the belief that there are parts of the Bible missing. There is research proving these theories, and it is decades old.

I have concluded that what we call churches are a product of man. I have not found any place in the Bible where God commanded a specific church to exist here on earth. The Bible does however state that we are the church, our bodies are the temple of Christ. It also encourages us to congregate together. I take this to mean "affiliate with people of like mind and spirit so as to keep us on track and not let the chaos of life bring us down."

When a building is filled with people who **have truly come together in the spirit** to worship a loving God, the energy (Holy Spirit) is overwhelming.

Therefore, giving the congregation the proof they need that God exists, by feeling His presence. During this time people's intentions are in right perspective. They have left their egos behind. For when human ego is present, so are their judgements, leaving no room for God's presence.

Religion contains politics, conditions, and the human need to control others. The love of God and Jesus Christ has no conditions or politics. Nor is it controlling. Their love is unconditional. It is my belief that religion is a tool (along with many others) that God has given the human race because they need proof that He lives (exists). It is also my belief that society has set so many rigid constraints concerning church, God, and Jesus Christ that real spirituality has been lost to politics and the human need to control others. Therefore, those who have no desire to be involved in such matters have stepped away and developed their own spirituality or faith. Meaning we've forgotten the true reasons for believing and remaining in right standing with God and Jesus Christ.

As for the contents of the Bible, it is not what is in our head that matters, it is what's in our heart that is important. We can read or memorize scriptures and doctrines until the cows come home, but it will not do us any good until our hearts receive and believe the message to be true. For our hearts to receive said message we first need to believe in a Higher Power/ God.

I have also concluded that God has sent me to school here on earth to learn all I can about being a loving and forgiving person. God created *everything* we know, all of which have a purpose. He created everything good and true in this world, the result being there is much to be learned concerning Him. It is up to us to be open minded enough to learn that which He has provided us with here on earth. However, it does not mean that we need to accept or apply those which do not work for us personally. Examples: Eastern cultures, Buddhism and its philosophy, Native American spirituality, Life Force Energy, Christianity, and Shamanism, just to mention a few. All the above were designed with spiritual intent. That which is good and helps us to become more like God. There is unity in diversity.

I believe that God created the many different religions and tools per se because there are many different cultures, containing many unique individuals with minds and hearts of their own, and not everything or one thing will work spiritually for every single person.

My spirituality (faith, beliefs) is what works for me; it gives me the courage to continue when times get rough or confusing instead of giving up. It's an alternative for seemingly hopeless situations. We just need to be willing to find an alternative and then take the first step by participating in it.

I pray that everyone may find the positives in each day no matter how insignificant, along with the following:

- Be able to find that little light at the end of the tunnel, a ray of hope.
- Know you have a right to be who you are, any time, at any place, when your intentions are in right perspective and only then.
- That you be able to laugh and experience the joys of life more and more each day.

I also pray that the message I have delivered has instilled a desire within you to find your own alternative and seek your own path. The one that is right and good for you. Again, there are many right and good alternatives out there; we just need to be willing to find and participate in one.

Be the best you know you can be!
Good luck and God bless on your new journey!

God's presence is like that
of a feather!

95

9 798889 211410 3